35940

DISCARD

⓭ DORLING KINDERSLEY *READERS*

Level 1

Level 2

Level 3

A Note to Parents

Dorling Kindersley Readers is a compelling program for beginning readers, designed in conjunction with leading literacy experts, including Dr. Linda Gambrell, Director of the School of Education at Clemson University. Dr. Gambrell has served on the Board of Directors of the International Reading Association and as President of the National Reading Conference.

Beautiful illustrations and superb full-color photographs combine with engaging, easy-to-read stories to offer a fresh approach to each subject in the series. Each *Dorling Kindersley Reader* is guaranteed to capture a child's interest while developing his or her reading skills, general knowledge, and love of reading.

The four levels of *Dorling Kindersley Readers* are aimed at different reading abilities, enabling you to choose the books that are exactly right for your child:

Level 1 – Beginning to read
Level 2 – Beginning to read alone
Level 3 – Reading alone
Level 4 – Proficient readers

The "normal" age at which a child begins to read can be anywhere from three to eight years old, so these levels are only a general guideline.

No matter which level you select, you can be sure that you are helping your child learn to read, then read to learn!

LONDON, NEW YORK, DELHI, PARIS,
MUNICH, and MELBOURNE

Project Editor Naia Bray-Moffatt
Art Editor Catherine Goldsmith
Senior Art Editor Cheryl Telfer
Series Editor Deborah Lock
US Editor Adrienne Betz
DTP Designer Almudena Diaz
Production Shivani Pandey
Jacket Designer Dean Price
Photographer Steve Gorton

Gymnastics Consultant
Christine Hopple

Reading Consultant
Linda Gambrell, Ph.D.

First American Edition, 2002
00 01 02 03 04 05 10 9 8 7 6 5 4 3 2 1
Published in the United States by DK Publishing, Inc.
375 Hudson Street, New York, New York 10014

Library of Congress Cataloging-in-Publication Data
Ganeri, Anita, 1961-
    First day at gymnastics / written by Anita Ganeri.
    --1st American ed.
        p. cm. -- (Dorling Kindersley readers. 1. Beginning to read)
    ISBN 0-7894-8512-5 -- ISBN 0-7894-8513-3 (pbk.)
    1. Gymnastics for girls--Juvenile literature.
    I. Title. II. Series.
GV464 .G36 2002
796.44'082--dc21   2001032599

Color reproduction by Colourscan, Singapore
Printed and bound in China by L Rex Printing Co., Ltd.

The publisher would like to thank the following for
their kind permission to reproduce their images: **Allsport**: 31

Additional photography: Roy Moller
Models: Rebecca Dennehy Megan Shields Jenna Eaton, Stacey
Eaton, Emma Gossington, Alistair Smith, Jessica Tancock, Fiona
Chung, Louisa Millar, Laura Hillier, Olivia Jones, Natalia Anderson,
Lyn Shields, Becky McCormack.
In addition, Dorling Kindersley would like to thank Margaret Miler
for all her help and advice and permission to photograph in her
gym club, The Leatherhead Gym Club, UK
All other images © Dorling Kindersley.
For further information see: www.dkimages.com

see our complete catalog at
www.dk.com

DORLING KINDERSLEY READERS

BEGINNING
1
TO READ

First day at gymnastics

Written by Anita Ganeri

A Dorling Kindersley Book

Jenny tugged at the sleeves
of her new leotard.
Her mom tied up her hair.

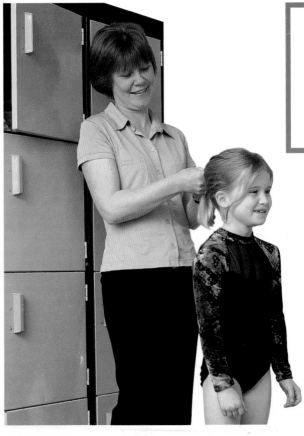

leotard

Jenny was going to gymnastics
for the first time.
What would it be like?

Anya had taken
gymnastics before.
"The class is really fun!"
said Anya.

The teacher was Ms. Sims.
She turned on the warm-up music.
The children hopped, skipped,
and jumped.

stretch

After that, they all stretched
their arms up in the air . . .

and then down to touch their toes.

"Spread out now
and find a big space on a mat,"
said Ms. Sims.
"Today Kate and Holly
will show you some moves.
We'll start with
a forward roll."

mat

Kate tucked in her head,
and pushed with her feet.
She rolled over.
Jenny did it
on her first try!

Next Kate did a backward roll.
Jenny did not find this so easy.
She couldn't turn over.

roll

"Put your hands by your ears,"
said Ms. Sims. "Now roll and push."

Kate then showed them
how to make different shapes
on the mat.
She lay on her back
and raised her arms and legs.

Then she lay on her belly
to make an arch.

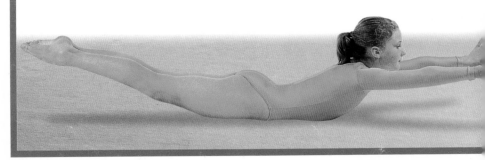

The class tried the shapes.
"Remember to stretch,"
said Ms. Sims.

Next Holly did a handstand.
She kicked her legs
up into the air.

Then Anya tried.
"Kick harder
and pull your legs together,"
said Ms. Sims.

Next Kate showed them
how to balance.
She lifted up one leg.

She stretched that leg
out to the side.
Then she stood
very still.

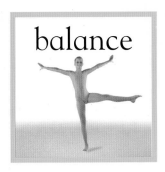

balance

The whole class
had a turn at balancing.
Jenny lifted one leg.
She tried to keep very still.
But it was hard not to wobble!

"You almost have it," said Ms. Sims.
"Hold out your arms
to help you balance."

The class split into groups next.
Anya and Jenny went
to the springboard
with their group.

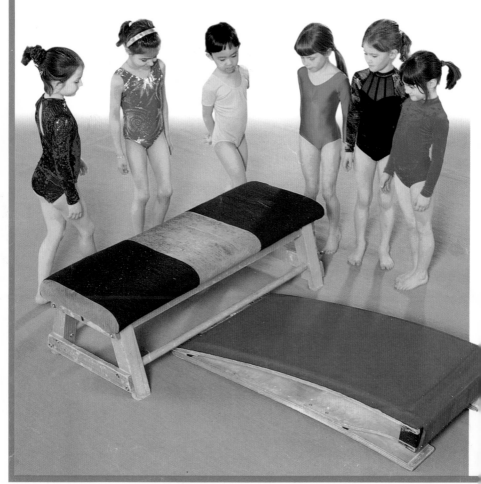

step

Holly showed them
how to step
onto the springboard
and jump off.

They went to the bars next.
Holly put both hands on the bar
and swung backwards
and forwards.
Then she let go and landed
on the soft foam below.

Ms. Sims lifted Jenny up to the bar and helped her to swing.

bars

Next, Holly climbed onto
the high beam.
She jumped up into the air
and bent her knees
as she landed perfectly.

beam

"You will be able to do that
when you are bigger,"
Ms. Sims told the class.
"First you must learn to balance
and walk on the floor beams."

Jenny walked carefully
along the floor beam.
She kept her back straight
and her arms stretched out.

Then she jumped off neatly.
"Very good, Jenny,"
said Ms. Sims.
"You have done well today."

The class was over.
"So soon?" Jenny said sadly.
Ms. Sims put on the music.

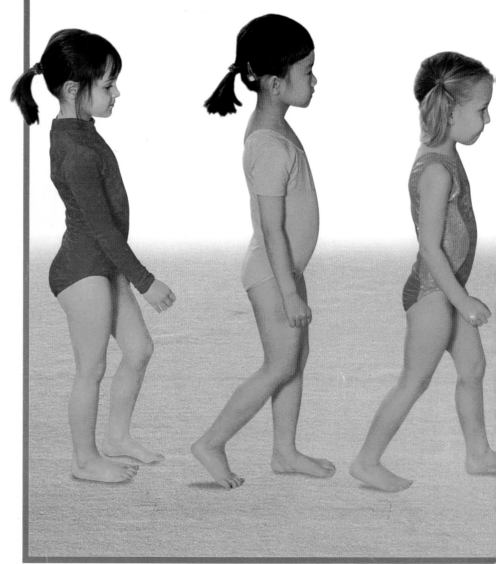

The children walked
in time to the music
and lined up to say goodbye.

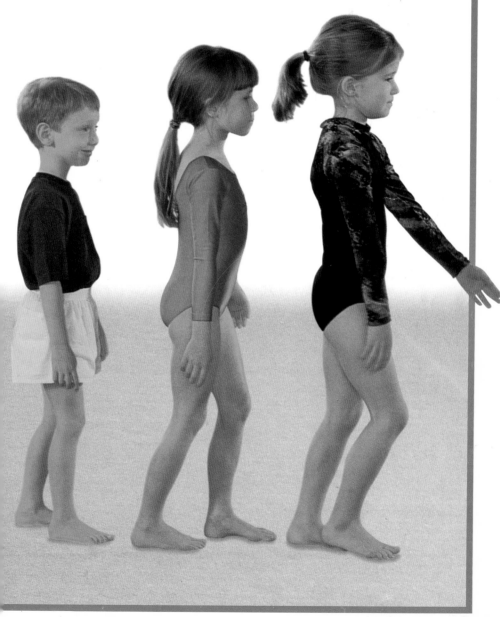

"Do you want to come again next week?" asked Jenny's mom. "Yes!" said Jenny.

One day I'll be a famous gymnast,
thought Jenny.
I'll balance on one leg.
I'll swing on the bars.
I'll jump on the high beam.
And I won't wobble!

Picture word list

leotard

page 4

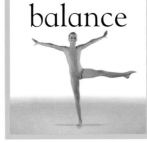

balance

page 17

stretch

page 7

step

page 21

mat

page 8

bars

page 23

roll

page 10

beam

page 24

DK DORLING KINDERSLEY READERS

My name is

I Gabo

I have read this book ✓

Date

GANVARY I